Also by Dixie Salazar

Altar for Escaped Voices
Blood Mysteries
Carmen and Chia Mix Magic
Flamenco Hips and Red Mud Feet
Hotel Fresno
Limbo
Reincarnation of the Commonplace
Voices of the Wind

CROSSHAIRS

OF THE ORDINARY WORLD

Dixie Salazar

STEPHEN F. AUSTIN STATE UNIVERSITY PRESS

For more information:
Stephen F. Austin State University Press
P.O. Box 13007 SFA Station
Nacogdoches, Texas 75962
sfapress@sfasu.edu
www.sfasu.edu/sfapress

Managing Editor: Kimberly Verhines

Cover art: "Synthesis" painted collage triptych

Distributed by Texas A&M Consortium
www.tamupress.com

ISBN: 978-1-62288-242-7

Acknowledgments

Grateful thanks to the editors of the following journals or magazines where these poems have appeared: *Triggerfish, Catamaran, Mirarmar, Salt, 2020, I-70 Review.*

For Zoe, Zack, Heather, John Shafer

And with much gratefulness to my friend and tireless, fearless fighter for social justice causes, Mike Rhodes. Also many thanks and great respect for those on the front lines: Nancy Waidtlow, Gerry Bill, Bev Fitzpatrick, Caroline Jackson, Art Dyson and many others.

CONTENTS

PART 3

Part 4

PART 1

Sheltering

My wisteria has abandoned
the arbor that sheltered us
summer nights as we toasted
another remembered summer night
a time of beer, blues and a broken leg
the story of our beginning
that now has come to an end.
And now the wisteria
refusing to die, has migrated
to the dead apple tree,
and taken up residence,
as a last resort.

In these dark days of isolation
I'm dancing alone now to my own
version of music- but together
we're all dancing in some form
to memories of yesterday's music.
"I Love you guys" drifts
over the neighbor's fence--
 I accept that alien pronoun
as one that could include myself.
"I love you too", I whisper to the fence slat.
OK OK OK a bird sings
from another neighbor's yard.

The Thing Is

We are here to laugh at the odds and live our lives so well that Death will tremble to take us. —Charles Bukowski
I'll think about that tomorrow. —Scarlet O'Hara

Here's the thing
we just keep putting
one under the influenced foot
in front of the other
seeing the Virgin Mary in tortillas
and romance in our pancakes
but we can't stop
the un-flattened numbers
120,000 and rising—even if
the naked emperor closes
his eyes so we can't see him
he says we'll be fine—
just don't think
about it and stop counting
for Christ sake!

So we just keep chewing and blinking
and charging our cell phones
wasting time as if it poured
from the spigots of endless wells--
listening to crickets
burble like aquariums
in the dark wet grass.
It's when they stop
that you have to worry--
waiting for death
to jump from the shadows
pull us into the cockpit
taking us up

into the cold, swallowing clouds.
They say we're in this together
which we are
but also we aren't; one day
we'll all be "alone again, naturally."

So we just keep searching for something
sweet and true to put in a sandwich
to wash down with a cold shot
of Southern dis-Comfort.
We keep searching for love
in all the wrong places--
say, where is the right place
to search for love?

Is it too much to ask
for someone to listen?
Is it too much to ask
for someone to lean into your space
and not even measure?
Is it too much to ask for truth
naked, elusive and beautiful?
tell me....

I think I'm getting it now
It is too much
Bring me another Scarlet O'Hara

Scarlet O'Hara recipe:

 1 ½ oz. Southern Comfort
1 ½ oz. cranberry juice
¾ freshly squeezed lime juice
Shake all ingredients with ice and strain into ice filled glass

Orpheus Laments

for Peter Everwine

He turns away from CNN
why didn't they listen?
he cries, posting a sad face--
hangs up his accordion
the last note wheezing
into the absence of footsteps
from the strip malls.
He won't accept your thoughts
and prayers or your Facebook
cry baby faces.
Last night swarms of hoarders
sheltered in Walgreen's
parking lot—this morning
there are no more Odor Eaters.
What are we to do now
with our stinking Nikes?
Action News announces
there is a shortage of harmonicas.
How will the Amish make music now?
Another tweet and the moon
has run out of ways to express disgust;
the insomniac rivers
lie awake in their tangled beds;
the birds in the Chinese elm only croak.
At five PM, all the neighbors open
their windows and howl
scaring the coyotes.
Our only hope lies
in rainbow hieroglyphics
chalked on sidewalks--
Whatever you do
don't look behind you.

One of Those Days

(Thanks to Eilen Jewel & the Beatles)

"One of those days"
when you find yourself choking
on the news
on the scene that rewinds
over and over where a choking
man begs for air-

when you can choke
on memories--
the girl who slept with a gun
under her pillow
she's still alive
"Time moves slow
and you lose control"
Manson hasn't found her yet.
They say he's dead
but she knows better.
He said there would be a war
didn't he?
"Get to the bottom
go back to the top…"
The drawn out anguish of a train
blows through your heart,
heavy cargo dragging down
the tracks....

rattle of the boxcars
one after another-- like
a scarred screen flashing

faces across—
"When grace seems far away"
a dark face on a milk carton
have you seen me?
You won't see me
I'm invisible--

There was a girl
in third grade, Phyllis--
held back two years,
but her body skipped ahead
to curves that only caused her grief,
taunts and whispers
that you took no part in
but neither did you stand up for her
and look…all these years later
you remember the pain
in those bottomless brown eyes.

There were witnesses
who watched the eight minute
flash of a life passing
there were cameras rolling…
"I can't face the day"
"One of those days"
when your mood ring turns black
and ashes from the burning cities
float helter skelter on the wind
"Get to the bottom
go back to the top…"
"I'm down beside myself"
A man walks out of the jail
in a paper suit, three dollars
in change in his pocket

he wrote a bad check
Rewind….he never walked out
he died on the street
calling to his mother—
 "Get to the bottom
go back to the top…"
This is not the world you dreamed of--

"One of those days"
when you find yourself choking
"your mind runs off to places
you can't go"
You're coming down fast
the light of a train barreling closer
all you need to do
is breathe.

On the porch
Listening

to sirens and the surf of traffic--
No one told us
the air could be this still
that you could hear the spaces
between bird cries
or the soft flapping
of leaves in the Gingko.
No one told us
that air ferns whisper
secrets even when no one
is there to hear.
If you sit still long enough
you can hear night approaching--
a lonesome moon
in a cold black bowl
where billions of stars live and die
with or without us.
No one told us time
could grind down
like a flattened stone
that whole days could drop
from the almanacs
and the aqueducts fill with tears.
In this new infected silence
I'm listening hard
for yesterday's band practice
that once drifted over the hydrangeas
for the street games of children--
but I think I hear coyotes
howling on the Golden Gate Bridge.

And now I hear the chop chop
of the crime copter lopping
circles around us from another
high speed chase in the neighborhood.
And laid over it all
the burbling coo of a morning dove
soothing its mate in the shadows
filled with shards of a shattered egg.

"Independent Ecstasy"

In the dark time, will
there also be singing?
Yes, there will also be
singing, about the dark time. —Bertold Brecht

When you are alone
you hear sounds
that may or may not be there
when you leave,
but you're not going anywhere
for awhile. The stages are dark,
the galleries locked,
the audiences dispersed
to I-pads and laptops.
But a low hum circulates
the heart of the house, as if
it is breathing or singing
in an undiscovered key.
You close your eyes
and surf the pulse beating
against the walls
under the stairwell
beyond the pantry, a buzzing
that breaks on the shore
of a bookshelf--
where the humming comes
from a dead poet
with an affinity for snakes
and baking bread
but yeast is scarce now
as Tylenol, toilet paper

and thermometers
and the snakes are posing with Bibles.
Her birds sang in trees
beyond applause or approval
un-witnessed, but for the
ecstasy within.
Sometimes it is all
there is…and you learn
to subsist on the wings
of a tree spread in the wind--
a child digging in the dirt
crafting whole colonies
from rocks and twigs.
She's alone, lost
in only the renown
of her own constructions
singing softly under her breath
in that shoreless place
beyond the edges of pain--
you know what I mean?
where time is a bird
flown out of its cage.

zoom

after ee c

hey everybody it's spring
everybody's zooming
and blooming with zoom cocktail
parties, zoom spelling bees,
therapy and mid year reports.
zoom zoom
it's spring and

poppies are popping
between spurge and cocklebur
equal bursts of foxglove
phlox and hairy nightshade
zoom
the stupidlyinlove doves
zoom, busy above
building unsafe nests in a hurry
to mate and incubate
zoom
hat riding backwards, the kid
sprung from school, zooms
by, his smile full of trouble
clicking the clickety-clack
cracks of the sidewalk
zoom
myownhummingbird zips
from one red cup to another
sucking up spring sweetness
zoom zoom zoom
the world ziplines by
a dizzy-dazzle-razmatz

of orange-red-butter-gamboge
fuschialicious- colors .
depending on us to be seen
and there on the lip
of a tender nasturtium
a snail
slipslidingalong carousing
in slime-lascivious glory
joining the blowoutorgy of
Spring!

Believe it Or Not

From here under the weakened stars
everything looks the same
but colonies of carpenter bees have been busy
sawing into the arbor, boring holes,
dropping chalky dust down onto my head--
tunneling deep inside the beams to lay their eggs--
while on an island near Paulu,
millions of moon jellyfish move close
to the surface of a lake, minus their sting
where they have been trapped
for centuries, mutated to survive
together with minimal oxygen.
Believe it or not
every inch of human skin
has 32 million bacteria…
Believe it or not
since tigers cannot purr, they show
happiness by squinting their eyes.
Believe it or not
In order to live in space a person
would have to drink 750 liters
of their own sweat and urine.
A day on Venus lasts 243 Earth days.
Tonight there's another Elvis sighting
in the hospital parking lot
where Gang of Youths tell us
the Heart is a Muscle and
sing of Strange Diseases.
Believe it or not
while hospital workers bag their gowns,
masks, gloves and stuff their shoes

into plastic bags at the end of their shifts,
worrying that an errant germ
might be riding in the folds of their earlobes,
heading home to temporary hotels,
they turn on the news to see
cars honking and circling the capital,
protestors hanging out the windows
with signs that say MY VIRUS MY CHOICE,
GIVE ME LIBERTY OR GIVE ME COVID
and I WANT A HAIRCUT.

Cold Pizza

I'm eating cold pizza for breakfast
in my sweats now for three days…
maybe it's lunchtime, not sure really.
Time is a snake swallowing its tail.
What day is it anyway?
Yesterday I wrote the wrong year
on a check, at least I think
it was yesterday. Oh yea,
it was the day my doorbell rang--
that was exciting.
Or maybe it was weeks ago
I think it was the day I talked for hours
with a friend about the past--
present and future turn into organ recitals now.
Isn't that what Alzheimers is like?
You forget the present and remember
the past in detail?
My dad, in his 90's, out of nowhere
recited a scene from Shakespeare's
Merchant of Venice. Maybe I have early onset….
No…I still remember who I am
and my children's names. Would anyone tell me
if I got them wrong? Or just humor me?
(Best not to upset her…)
the calendar's empty
the phone never rings… where are the telemarketers
when you need them?
I dreamed I was in prison last night
or was it the night before?
I had to get a number to line up for food
and stand on an X…wait…

maybe that really happened…
In the dream the food was all gone
when I got to the front of the line
but there was cake. And then I woke up
hungry…or did I wake up?
If I did wake up, I should go take a shower
but I think I already took one
so maybe that means I woke up…I guess…
Is it too early for a glass of wine?
Or maybe it's too late…where did
all these empty bottles come from?
Maybe I'll go for a walk
and wave to strangers
but I'm tired. Maybe I already walked today…
Hint for the day:
If someone comes toward you in a mask,
don't offer them all your money.
Sometimes I catch myself
staring into space for no reason…
does that count as meditation?
Wish I had a piece of cake right now.
Why is there a slice of cold pizza
on my coffee table?

Enough is Enough

Today the skies are full
of virus clouds like cirrus
only highly contagious
and flyovers that bathe
us in gratitude and carbon dioxide.
And the dog's chew toy
is virus shaped
the cat's hairball has spikes
the whoopee cushions
fart out puffs of tweets
waffles are just
another conspiracy theory
and the grandmas and joggers
are no longer safe—
and "fine people" are blocking
the ambulances
demanding their freedom
to spread disease
and lynchings are now
recorded on cell phones.
Enough is enough--
today I want to sing
like Leotine
dance like Josephine
blow my harp
jig like a drunken sailor
on infinity shore leave.
Today I want to turn
my "Kind of Blue" "So what" back
on all this noise
and belt out in Nina's voice
USA God Damn
at the top of my
fucking lungs!

Covid Jazz

Bring on the virus!
No, really, bring it on...
we gotta embrace it
or at least a second cousin
twice removed—or it'll kill us.
"Just a little bit"
Aretha would know.
We're not talking herd immunity either.
While you're at it
bring on syncopation--
jump off the beat!
Hit the 2 and the 4
hard and harder
short circuit the frontal lobe
go ahead-- get possessed
by jazz and voo doo rhythms--
give us a therapeutic dose
of that primeval poison
"that old black magic"
flatten the curve with
the flatted fifth.
Give in to Green Chimneys,
black neutron stars,
and Thelonius wrinkles in space.
Go into the mass gap--
and expect the unexpected
down at the invisible crossroads
of immortality and mortgaged souls--
just get down and groove!
Bring on organized chaos--
let me take you

on a covid cruise.
Think outside the space/ time
continuum--
every theory has some uncertainty
everything's gonna be allright
syncopate and inoculate--
it's all about the count--
one and a two and a -- hit it!

Prayer for the Pandemic

I am not religious
so I don't pray
but lately, sitting under the arbor
with tequila and a wedge of moon
when Dr Fauchi says it's safe
and the index is stacked
in our favor, I've felt
my lips moving, felt another breath
enter my breath- exhaling
me to distant skies
not uglier than toenail fungus
but more believable than relics
and believers who have become relics.
Some things you can't fake--
guess I just don't have that Jesus chip
but at least I'm not praying for money
which should be a sin, let's say it is
and my hands are happy birthday clean

and I can have a staring contest
with the Q Anon cucumbers
that never ripened
I won't look away
and I can twist and shout
at the newest conspiracy headline
or climate denier's prayer
for lamb's blood to wash it all away--
while the bloated sun
hangs red behind curtains of ash
drifting up from the fire blistered hills.
In the shadows there are drums
thumping and harmonicas

bent to hell and back.
All together now--
Are you ready to dance and sing?
You can't carry a tune?
Let it carry you
where you need to be--
staring into the eye of a storm with
no moral center—don't look away
laugh, sing, dance
all are ways of praying.

PART 2

All Those Blazing Headlines

make it hard to chew, swallow, floss
whistle, to slip into a dress
sprigged with buttercups,
to accept another moment of silence
to bend to another prayer, a voice
from the void, from the bottom
of a sea of graves.
Someone coughs
someone turns a page or runs
a red light—life goes on, right?
Or does it?
Does it pelt us again with stats
or stall in the left turn lane
and wait to be towed to an empty lot?
I want to believe in birds
and buttercup moons--
I want to keep the window
to my heart open to let the wonder
in with carbon fumes, wind,
and night perfume but
there's a hole in the sky and spent
shells scattered in the orchards, a lone
man deep in the shadows, pockets
heavy with a cold, hard darkness
that cannot be outrun.

Shootout at the Wonderland Car Wash

Two concealed carry permit holders
shoot and kill each other in Michigan.

Soapy slick, the parking lot is swept clean now
of yellow tape and bullet casings.
Attendants fly white flags of detail rags,
pull straws, soda lids and stained receipts
from the gunnels where a line of tires will nest,
feeding car after car into the mouth
of the tunnel that swallows equally
the CEO, the high school dropout and the mother
hushing her three year old, who screams in terror
at the blotting darkness, the roar, the swish
of monster brushes clawing the windows,
at the blaze of light barreling toward him
from the tunnel's open jaw.
Hush now, she brushes
his hair, assures him it's OK, nothing to
be frightened of… as the conveyer rail
delivers them once again whole, safe and sound
into the hungry crosshairs of the ordinary world.

Wild Geese Over Grocery Outlet

Weeks go by with no breathable air
eyes hungry for untamed green
wild for landscapes off track and grid.
Shopping carts rattle and clang
waiting for high fructose, saturated
fat and whipped plastic
to fill their wide, steel bellies.

No one looks hungry here
as if they could go for weeks, live
off cellulite and spare tires
while carts stack high
with Screaming Hot Cheetos
and mutated pancakes
from some laboratory in Asia.

While fleets of silver carts
with burping wheels roll down
the aisles, starvation is setting in—
persistent gnawing that leaves us
frantic for substance, weak
for leafy greens, smoky sage
pine or flash of feathers.

But when we roll out the flapping doors
and strain against crooked wheels
our eyes lift over Arbys and Motel 6
to an arrow of wild geese
shooting through the clouds
the icy stars and day glo vapors
hunger winging us all forward.

Jogging at VSP*

Even though I round the dirt track
again-- always watching behind
for fist or shiv, I'm running against
myself—against the thirty years
that have brought me to cinders
under foot, burnt tire smells in the
air, the wounded bull horn buzzer
bleating over the yard.
The sun spins in the clouds
like my dreams of suffocating
in the bleached undies of convicted felons—
choked by state issued muh muhs
when I slip into the pile of laundry
swallowed by soap scum
and high suds of regret.
One more lap
and the morning moon rises
and sails through yard recall as if
that tiny speck of light flickering
up from what might as well be Mars
could spell anything fresh, new or
unstained, as if this dark ring
pounded into the earth by
fallen angels could ever offer
anything more than another
dull slap of mother earth under
the punishing thump of these feet
that have carried me in circles
inside circles that have come so close
to flight, almost touching the sun.

Valley State Prison, Chowchilla

View from the Asylum

...the sadness will last forever. —V. Van Gough

Starry Starry Night hums on FM
radio in my car at Trader Joes.
I'm crying over spilled colors, over
the effort to keep disintegration
at bay --and the high price of some kind
of belief in the worth of this sad life.
Sunflowers explode from foil, ready
for purchase like most of what you see
prices slashed – sale- sale –shining
out, like a carnival barker's mustache—
skies tagged with mark down clearance.
Every corner-- a carnival of chickens
break dancing-- and skating bananas who
twirl signs while competing for pennies of
attention-- pushing pizzas, hearing aids
implants and gold. Hydrangeas buzz blue
smashing into yellow zig zags of
neon from a parking lot Ferris wheel's
chrome yellows and cobalt blues--
cart-wheeling against the night sky,
coiling and clanging like museum
alarms, shorted out with the overload
of pigment and pure sensation when
the tourists have all gone off to bed.

A girl in hot yellow shorts trolls Blackstone
flicking ashes, thinking this is the day
someone will listen, will pay what she's
worth-- while around the corner waits the bag

of sadness she'll settle for. Her eyes
are painted big as sunflowers to snag
the right buyers, but behind the blue
irises, an ember still smolders like
Vince's eyes sizzling in memory
from the museum walls, the speck that
won't go out, a bulb deep in permafrost,
waiting to thaw around a blue flame
that no one sees, the tiniest crack of
thawing that no one hears, the last note
of the song played at Tupac's funeral.

The sunflowers, the bananas, the girl
won't make it, but the sadness will last
forever--as long as the ring of
 the auctioneer's hammer at Sothebys.
He could never imagine this when he
learned to get by on smells of cobalt and
boiled roots-- a few flecks of hot Gamboge—
all that's left when the tills clang shut at night.

Exhuming Neruda

Leave me in the midst of my own moon, in my wounded terrain.

Maybe if you just know one thing
it's enough.
Pick one thing
like a seahorse or leaf
to study, to sing
for the rest of your life—
examine its history
eons ago with the first
uncoiling-- the first whisper
and all it carried--
a swirl of leaves sailing
on forever into mist and music--
boats that never dock
that sag in the river
the moon plows through
then rocks on the shore
of your heart
while the stars stumble and fall
down the broken stairs
of eternity.

Black crepe crackles
in the fire of blossoms
and drunken trees
sing off key and gallop
into the ruins.

Even the gutters run
with green ink;
fish scales chime on the wind
then sway into silence one by one.

Let the shovels clang,
hit hard pan and permafrost
all they'll find are blackened salt,
fish bones, a needle with broken thread,
and the charred strings
of a gutted guitar--

music cannot be exhumed--
Everything carries you to us.

St Judas Tadeo (Saint Judas of Thaddeus)

(liked by narcos, the patron saint of lost causes).

Wouldn't you love to have a patron saint
of all that's bad for you, that you
can't give up? He or maybe she would
not only let you drink, sleep, eat, buy,
and indulge to extreme in every pleasure
but applaud your wildest impulses.
Buy the Jimmy Choos! Punch the accelerator,
eat the frozen birthday cake at 2 AM.--
kiss the blue eyed snake of excess.
Saint Tadeo, Saint Judas of Thaddeus
is your guy…the patron saint of lost
causes. But of course there's a catch.
Light a candle in the chapel of no
tomorrows and quicksand
guilt. Unless you can strike some
kind of bargain with Tadeo like the narcos
must do when they call on his help for
stealing crops. What do they offer
in return when there's no reserve in
the soul's already mortgaged account?
What do they tell themselves
in that raw moment just before sleep
when it's one on one, without
even a feather of denial between them
and the imagined listener?
Do they spin the wheel of borrowed excuses
and tired justifications?
Or do they crack open a beer with Saint T
kick back, call up the old days
when apologies were only for the weak--
reassure T it's OK to be an underachieving saint
and make another promise to make it
all right in the end.

Plenty

Our table holds plenty--
lace draped old oak laden
with fruits fallen from the
red skies of October--
pomegranates, sour green
apples, persimmons, shine
with life that also holds
plenty of pepper sized
creatures crawled in from the
cold, trying to survive--
specks, some invisible
they dance ecstatically
seeking warmth as we all
do. And yet…a warm hearth,
scarlet rubies bursting
and splattered Pollock like--
staining lips with juice and
Bonnard reds-- puckered for
fruit kisses ripening
on a cobalt plate-- feast
for eyes and mouths, we fill
ourselves and yet…it is
never enough. We need
more invisible wings
blending ochre and wild
red, primary couplings
that feed the gaps in us--
as old as the stories
of hot yellow bile and
cold black, and the old need
to balance the humors

to hold dark in one hand
light in another and
know that plenty alone
can never be enough.

Green Arrow

Today I wanted to write a poem
that smelled like hibiscus in Spring, but when
I opened my window, the smell of manure
drifted in, like you mash into raised beds
and later watch fat juicy tomatoes
jump out of the ground overnight.
I wanted a poem like finely spun silk
but when I pushed back my chair it caught on
a hairball coughed up by the cat, so I
closed my eyes but all I could see was
the face of the girl on the median at
Palm and Shaw with her pleading sign.
I didn't even give her a dime
because I didn't want to dig in my
purse and I was in a bad mood and I
missed the green arrow and thought about that
leftover sushi waiting at home, and
what if I had to stand on a corner
holding up a sign just to get a greasy
corn dog from the AM PM mini mart
and then I felt awful and wanted
to give her a buck but the light changed and
I couldn't hold up the line, so I raced
home in time for the mail, a funeral
insurance ad in Spanish and a letter
from the cousin of an African
emperor who'd recently died, but the
cousin couldn't get all his millions and
needed my bank account now so he could
split the money with me a complete
stranger…which for some reason made me think

of Billie Holiday's song…yea, I'd like
to write a poem like that…sweet, acidic—
then, strange blessing, the doorbell rang. Through the
screen door, the Virgin Mary was selling
rib eye steaks from a van. I was in luck—
God Bless the Child That's Got His Own, I said
and shut the door, the smell of manure

lingering, even sweeter than before.

Searching for Light

Darkness has overtaken light
melted into coppery pools
that drain away with every headline
and newscast. Floods, fires,
tyrants, earthquakes, cancer,
murders, hurricanes, massacres,
pandemics, books written in blood.
When I open my eyes
each day, the light bulbs in their sockets
have dimmed a little more—
my own burden of darkness not
lessened or lifted even a little.
Each night the house fills
with darkness and in the morning
the darkness lines have risen
another notch up the walls--
soon there may be no difference
when I open my eyes
or close them. Soon, the dark birds
that close their wings around the moon
may swoop down, gather
and swallow the last remains of light.

But in the middle of a night
with no moon, a night pulsing
with heaviness
and a scratching at the door
something trying to get in or escape--
I awake from a bed of burning boats
to the afterimage of a circle of light
fighting to enter like the first breath
of a baby waiting to be born.

PART 3

Danger Zones

Anyone biking through these smog choked streets
pocked with holes that could swallow a squirrel
knows the dangers-- the blur
of speeding machines inches away
whooshing through peripheral space
the sense that any second
on this ordinary day
we could all end in a pileup of twisted metal.

Anyone biking past the shuttered library
on another day of counting bodies
can see the homeless stranded outside --
shopping carts parked in a circle
like the Donner party.
Today, no one's checking out
The History of Infectious Diseases
or The Best of Science Fiction 2020.
Today we are living it.

Anyone biking past Dirty Bird Laundry
would not smell the soapy sweetness today--
it is not an ordinary day of suds, rinse, spin.
And at Funky Shack (smokes and clothes),
I imagine smoke ruffling up from rounders
of cheap synthetic kaftans
a stampede of bargain shoppers, their pockets
filled with rolling papers and pipes
essential services, for today.

Anyone biking past Channel Breeze apartments
with no channel or breeze could catch

a whiff of gamey discarded recliners
wafting up from the sunken
ribs of shopping carts and mossy tires
in the canal whose sparkling face
gives no hint of the sucking current below.

On past Casa Elegante – stucco, sprayed
with graffiti, past Hidden Gardens
I dare you to find them.

Now…Entering another zone where every day
invisible spores flutter in the whirr of
hummingbirds and dance on doorknobs,
I wake in the darkness—
my heart, a runaway horse
the rain is calling me home
the moon has misplaced the tides--
But what I fear the most
is the child who offers
a hand that I am afraid to touch.

Ordinary Magic

Beneath a sky sized neon hand
Mrs. Day, palm reader of Highway 99
divines the shape of sunlight
on the grackle's wing
studies the broken life line of the snail's
trek over gravel flecked
with the sparks of stars.

When travelers have eaten their fill
of number four, Klein's Truck Stop Special,
chosen White Shoulders or My Sin
from the ladies, or colored condoms
from the men's room,
they will park Winnebagos by the rose trellis
and ask Mrs. Day to fathom
their folded up dime store hearts—
to forecast the romance
of chipped fingernail polish
and reveal to them their true
Egyptian midnight selves.
She'll gaze into stale coffee dregs
and pools of rainbowed gasoline
and read futures of perfect bowling scores
and early paroles.

But when neon blue spells "closed"
Mrs. Day enters the almond sweet air,
black orchards where owls
digest the fallen stars.
Then heavy rigs hum
with the buzz of power lines

and Mrs. Day need not predict
the six car pileup on Interstate Five,
the oil spill off Badger Pass Road,
the sudden unexplained violence
of the bloated moon.

She'll trail the owl's path of pellets
through wet vineyards on back roads
past "Rifles Made to Order"
and beyond the Bluebird Motel,
in the pastel aura of mushrooms and gnomes
she'll trace the cryptic shadows
of her lover's eyelids,
the one who asks nothing
from the moon's light circling her eyes,
who demands no Powerball visions
or shooting star predictions
but melts with her in the ordinary magic of touch
and the simple alchemy of love.

Lucky Strike

If you're traveling south on highway 41
doesn't matter where you're going
or where you've been

if you're caught in the desolation
of this place where tractors
and oleanders rust together

and a coppery patina dusts even
the yellow weeds that flow on for miles
as the sun settles into a fiery blaze

of lazy pollen and vehicle exhaust,
you can't help but soak up
the alkaline despair of battered dreams.

You speed past loaves of hay
crusting in a field; a power plant
scaffolds the sky around signs

for Cherry Auction Swap Meet
and radar enforced speed zones
with not a plane in sight.

A tumbleweed lifts straight upward,
floating like an exotic bird
or a religious apparition

settling down by King's Rest Motel
with nothing but vacancies
and running toilets.

You can't help but wonder
how it would be to work swing
at the Grab n Go,

pushing change across a scarred counter
bagging cigarettes and Slim Jims
chirping have a nice day

every wrist slitting moment
of an eight hour shift that runs
into perpetual overtime when Ricky,

the relief checker calls in sick
once again because his uncle
dies over and over

and his kid breaks the same
arm over and over
and Ricky falls off the wagon over and over.

Your supervisor heads to the
parking lot with her Luckies, croaking again
how she's not gonna do this forever.

But when you punch out, there's a moon
like a curved minnow swimming
upstream through a bank of clouds

riding the neon currents and feral glow
of TV lights winking on here and there
in a foamy sea of almond blooms.

You pass that happy bitch
up there in the sky, all lit up,
flashing her Table Mountain winner's face

all over a field of rotting cars.
You go home to the double wide
with the collapsing shed—

you fall asleep to the chilling howl
of dogs packed up and chasing the moon.
You thrash in your twisted sheets

to the rise and fall of an endless
line of big rigs churning past
the wink of lanterns

up and down darkened canals
where they set up their cool chests
and fish for catfish, striper and carp

living the lives none of them expected,
waiting all night under the cold stars
for that first quick punch of a lucky strike.

The Tower Talks

with thanks to Chris Stapleton

Come back, come back
the mannequins are lonely
sheltered in the darkened windows
of La Tienda Thrift, gathering
dust and silverfish.
Fab is silent, dazed in purple
expectation of throbbing rhythms
that have disappeared
with the sequins, feathers
and skin tight electronic Lycra.
All the recliners at International
Furniture have gone into permanent
recline, waiting… with everyone else
waiting with ghosts of the bouncers
at Lucy's Lounge, hunched over
their cell phones… waiting
for a nonexistent Friday night.
The clocks at Tower Clock Shop
have all run down, the hours
and minutes sliding into the by and by
with stray meteor dust from stars
that died a million years ago.
Marilyn is trapped on the side
of a building with a pirate
asking where is the music;
where are the lovely strung out angels
with their broken halos?
Where are my alcoholics, my hipsters,
my beer a day for life investors
in the Sequoia Loggers Club?

Where are the dragons?
They have escaped
from the Dragon's Treasure
setting fires in the parking lot
of the Tower Theatre where the marquee
displays a memorial service
from a month ago, when my streets
were full of stolen shopping carts
tattooed dropouts and bipolar vets laughing
in their collars at inside jokes.
All that's left now is a man
sleeping on a bench beside
his Lactose Intolerant milk carton,
an almost empty bus huffing by
with words on the side:
"I Don't Know, Do You?"

Meditations at Three AM

If it's three AM
and you're awake like I am
you might hear appliances grumbling
in a minor key-
or cranky floorboards ticking off
every creak and groan of sore old bones
or the snickering of lactose intolerant mice
who sneer at your traps
then poop and nest in your t-towels.

Your memory switches on
like a manic Klezmer violinist on meth--
what if you had married that Portuguese sheep farmer
with the silver blue Buick Skylark?
What if your dad had invested in property
on the coast instead of Lodi?
Maybe you shouldn't have ordered that
folding nose trimmer, curling iron, flashlight combo.

Now you're rewinding
back to third grade
a parade of humiliations--
Mrs. Umfer reading aloud to the class
the love note Richie Spengler sent you--

Onto things you should have said--
no I will not babysit your Siamese cat
a known canary stalker
and yes, the worst happened
a crime scene of blood and feathers--
or "screw your downward dog, upward cat, cobra

cow, lion your whole zoo of hypocrite poses"
to the namaste bumper sticker
who cut you off in the Whole Foods parking lot.

Now you compose a letter to the editor
about the misuse of bike lanes
the wrong way upstream riders and heavy breathing
mask-less walkers plowing into your path from behind.

If it's after three AM
the moon is a round, white flag
surrendering to Conan and TCM--
you want nothing more
than the cold cock of oblivion
the sweet amnesia slip-stream
of unconsciousness.

You pray to the Tiki lamp
for sweet, Titanic Tsunami sleep
to engulf you
but now all the words
for Sweet Home Alabama
are jolting through your brain--
if only there was an on/off switch
there should be an off switch--
design flaw you think hearing
the spit and sizzle of a June bug
velcroed to your pillow.

If "Jesus Just Left Chicago"
at "Nighttime on The City of New Orleans
with fifteen cars and fifteen restless riders
three conductors and twenty-five sacks of mail,"
how many "Red Rubber Balls"

would it take to sink
a "Yellow Submarine?"

If it's past three AM
and you're still awake,
call me....
we'll start that sagging panty hose support group-
or we'll deconstruct Proust's Complete, Unabridged
Remembrances of Things Past
or maybe we'll just listen to each other's
heavy breathing until one of us falls asleep.

Blackberry Moon

for JS

Maybe you didn't know
that tulips can smile
or that blackberries can fly
waiting in the darkness
for a signal form the conductor
of perfectly ripe moments
purple-black like the eyes
of a dog, panting in the moonlight
waiting for a warm and familiar weight.
Berries, plump and big as the dog's nose—
moist, furry and warm.
The dog will wait
as long as it takes.
Everything waits
and waits
for the moon's signal
lifting with light and readiness—
the heart of a tulip opens--
the blackberries soar.

PART 4

Open Your Eyes

after Phil Levine

I found a whole apple pie in the dumpster
took it back to share with one of my moms
and the rest of the camp. Then I walked
through the early evening smoke
where dust and smog scribbled the sky a fiery rose
and muddy canal waters gathered reds and pinks
and spread them out in watery scarves.
From behind the silos, stray gulls rose
and winged into a sunset that opened wide
to darker and deeper purple reds that just
screamed louder and louder --look
look at this wealth of colors
spread over the cracked earth.
Open --wider and wider- to streaked skies
fall down in the soft dirt--
to praise the sun dropping over the rim
of the world and breathe in the fire
no matter how many curses the man
behind food Max screamed after you --no matter
how many signs the city has posted
evicting you from your absence of a home.

There are some things that cannot be found
on E-Bay, appraised, amortized stolen or seized
by men in orange vests when they come to bulldoze
our beds and inventory our weary forks and spoons
to store them in bins with the rats and maggots--
some things are right and true and cannot
be sullied by words dressed up in official seals,

the simple joys that don't break down in
either the grind of use or neglect.
My second Mom and I came to this, sharing pie
with Chuey and Wayne in a patched tent
beside a canal open to the raggedy wind.

If you don't believe me...
open your eyes and see
dark shapes moving through the shadows
pushing everything they own from one corner
of the city to another- hidden from nothing—
not even eyes that attempt to hide--
open your eyes and also
that parched, dry place where you pledge
allegiance to money and pat your wallet
for reassurance --open your eyes
to a skinny bird stripping a carcass
quietly in a parking lot as the sun drips down
sharing what's left of its meager light
into clumps of Ailanthus, the tree of Heaven
that some would say are not even trees.

One paycheck

Once I owned a house in Old Fig--
magical garage doors,
mirror tiles etched with unicorns
sparkly granite counter tops
with wall to wall debt and black mold
seeping through the baseboards.
At work I made coffee for big shots
typed up reports, lied to their wives
and trolled E Bay by night.
It was a good life I thought
even with the wobbles.

Now I push a wobbly shopping cart
filled with all I own—today, that is…
before it's stolen or grabbed by the cops-- pots
for boiling Top Ramen, rusted hot
plate, ragged toothbrush, stained pillows
and a cigar box where I keep my secret stash
wrapped in velvet—fish, giraffe,
flamingo, octopus, swan all spun
from glass and the best one
a unicorn-- for when I get really hard up.
Yesterday, I traded a seahorse for tampons.
Sitting, propped against the cart and morning
glories, I watch a soft wind sifting
through the car wash, picking up plastic bags
and yellowed sales slips from the thrift store
think of the rows of used clothes, the racks of shoes,
the shelves of dishes, candles and books
the stuff of our lives, old and new becoming
old before they're out of the box. I wrap my arms

around this old army coat, let the sun
swaddle me, soak through the layers
embrace all that's survived--
all that's discarded-

Intro to Physics

This morning because little waves of potential
heart beats are bumping
together, Sinamen crosses from Winchell's
doughnuts to Denny's pushing a stroller of Top
Ramen, heart pills, everything else the cops
haven't taken yet—topped by a small
refrigerator and sock monkey, twerking
a red butt to the late for work
red light runners—she takes her time, smelling
sweet maple buns and burnt tires
folded together—hearing a school yard bell
ring somewhere nearby, the children spilling
out in waves for recess, freed from the lazy,
droning Intro to Physics, laughing
and smacking a tether ball
up to a ghost moon, only there
like a fingerprint dusted after a crime--
a spree of crimes everywhere--
seen and unseen. In her pocket, unspent,
the quarters lie quiet and tired
in yesterday's lint,
no longer needed for the phone call
she thought about this morning
when she first woke under the tall
shrubs along the railroad
tracks and remembered like a lightening
bolt to the heart, the cold window
where sparrows sing differently now
as if they know
they are unobserved.

Happy Hour

(after Neruda) for Sinamen

Just because the canal reveals undigested innards
of mud-spoked Big Wheels, shopping carts spangled
with hospital bands & lost baby teeth--
Just because morning groans the cracked song
of an old man's barnacled spine--
none of this means I can't be happy
can't count the drops of birthday wishes
circling in the gutter
can't sing about love and mashed potatoes
or watch a burning window
collect hot reds from a sunset.
"Today let me be happy"
allow my feverish feet
to skip over the worm castings of sorrow
hide from the homeless police
float above mosaics of broken glass
where the wind is a lucky bump
to see me through the saddest hours
of home cooked pass the salt wounds
with extra helpings of shattered kisses.
Allow me to surf through ecstatic smog
with my girls around me
warning of meteor shark attacks
barking at stray memories that come barreling
out from under the aqueduct as if to drown
this miracle of a day
when some official somewhere decides
to open the sluice--
just let me take wing on the backwash

and something close to a song leak through my teeth
as if it is enough
as if I had some part
in the making of this sweet tragedy.

Above and Below

I'm on the roof of a boarded up house
the only place safe
from voices seeping from manholes
and from under the fake walls
of my caseworker's office
and because PG&E sent workers
to clog the vents with poison smoke
and now won't return
my calls. It took all my strength
to climb up here beside the deflated
reindeer and the crumbling chimney
but from here I can see the tops
of dusty magnolias, the stains of
falling stars on the cement below
and watch the entry ports..

I flip a Bic on off on -- watch
its flame eclipse the sun sliding
under a row of oleanders where my girls
wait, Shaunti leaking a soft growl,
Sheba ready to tear open
the throat of anyone approaching
my invisible fence.

When the day moon signals all clear
I pack up what hasn't been stolen
or lost -- head out with my girls
who dance around the bubble I walk inside of
along the canal, nipping
at stray tails of wind.

Once, at home, I lived under the house
curled up like a hermit crab,
letting the daily explosions
crash over me, loving the smell
of aloneness, mildew and wet cement.
She came down pointing her finger
"why aren't you a doctor and you
don't have to live like this."
I watched swarms of her words
cut off by the surf
of whispering gnats that drew ever closer.

Now they follow me, beseeching
me to pray for forgiveness from above
or to push back the devil's rat pack
but I've flown up to the clouds
and I've slept in the shadows and lint of his pocket
and I'm not afraid of them
only the ones who have touched me
and my girls in between
and left their marks.

Now I'm roaming with my girls- seeking
a vacant alley, an overlooked spot along the tracks
an empty bush—a welcoming culvert
where we can all lie down and let the stars
fall into our eyes, seeking forgiveness
over and under the house but never inside--
alive between concrete and constellations.

Blues for Big Sue

*for Sharen Bobbitt, died 12/28/11 on the sidewalk
in front of Poverello House, a homeless shelter.*

She jumped from box to box, chalked
on the sidewalk, jumped from box to box
rolled her stones like bones-- forecast

a future of striped socks and holly hocks
yea, the wind sang holly hocks... but box
car blues jumped the moon and tracks

who could know that little girl who'd grow
that little girl who'd grow--they'd throw
her bones so far away from home—

Law come and chalked her passway with an X
yea, they laid a crossmark where she lay
herself to rest-- left her shoes- soul they hauled away

Captured her foot tracks-- steel jaws snapped
even memories-- when she stepped on a crack
and bulldozers broke her mother's back

 They shut down the sidewalk
crushed the moon-- forced from box to box
till she laid out cold as the heart of a stopped clock

who could know that little girl would grow
wings when she lay in the cold—or that they'd sow
her bones so close, so far away from home

"chalked her passway with and X, lay a crossmark where she lay, captured
her foot tracks" voo doo references familiar to Southern blues musicians.

At the crossing

Time changes us, but do we change
time? Yellow leaves turn red despite
us and our hunger for speed or
pixil records of our latest
meal, proving matter does exist--
we've seen it on Facebook. But each
morning sky spills light onto our
heads, and more birds than we can know
the names of swing out of the trees
with no need for password or pin
number. The days whoosh by like a
passenger train's mirage of lit
windows with people full of thoughts
whirling faster than the speed of
light. Flashing away, it drags its
heavy cargo of consciousness
leaving a big hole in the night.

Night Music

At night, shopping carts come out
with the moon, click clack click clack;
rattle and clang—a chain
gang of carts bumping over the tracks.
Lights wink up and down the street
like fireflies dipping into broken glass.

When the moon rocks alone
in the night, the stars wink out one by one
making a music heard only by those
covered in fish scales
who shake marbles in rusted tin cans,
dig through burnt out light bulbs
smashed aluminum
ham bones and tossed egg shells
crowding around open bins,
sparring for copper and tin
while Bone Thugs, 96 Tears
and Maybe This is Home fade
into the night with the bent wail
of a train's last breath.

Hope

for Phil Levine who always gave us hope.

In the alley of weeds
and puncture vines, a hole
in the fence slat opens
to a vista of more
weeds and earth sucked dry of
moisture and nourishment,
a lone tomato vine
struggles to lift the just
opened eyes of wet stars
seeking the sun's blessing—
and quiet miracle
of touch from a woman,
crusted with layers of
dirt, sun baked, much like the
same earth she plows with
her broken spoon. Every
morning and night, she pours
water from a Bud Light
and clears away goat grass,
stink weed and spurge—while Eve
and Lil Bit guard her stuff
back at the encampment.
Hope is not a place she
visits often now, not since
the news arrived second-
hand –the worst a mother
can imagine—and then
spotlights at night, jerking
them from sleep—their blankets

sleeping bags stripped away
leaving them to gather
warmth from whatever stray
body they can press against
leaving them to curse the
stars that claw through filthy
clouds, offering them not
even one spare wish to
shine in a gutter, to
toss in a dark canal
and sink with the muddy
moon— not even a wish
so small, it could slip through
a razor blade's eye or
the spaces of static
on the cop's radio
when he returns two
hours later to bark
another warning to
move on, not seeing the
finger she shows his back
or the Bud Light she smashes
against the fence—hard boil
inside, all she has left--
it has to be enough
she thinks, watching the stars
of glass burst like fireworks
in the night. Hugging herself
for warmth, there's plenty more
always plenty more for
morning, to empty and
refill with water or
strafe the burial grounds of
wishbones and fallen stars.

This Moment

If you don't stir your soul with a stick every day, you'll freeze solid.
　　　—Tom Van Deel (a borrowed epitaph)

This moment when nothing is in its usual place
where nothing stays and the wind chases

plastic bags across an empty parking lot
where rats feast on the rot

of sardine remains and tossed chow mien
and crickets tune up for a concert to no one

listening in the darkened galleries
no one braving this covid-cold and rain to see

there overhead, thousands of white wings
against the black window of night--starlings

exploding with cries that startle
the empty streets, empty but for the wheelchair

where a homeless man rolls a joint by
cellphone light and the empty number twenty-five

whooshes by with a gasp
of dazed light in a darkened galaxy

There is nothing
more than this moment.

October Rain- Stanford

for J.S.

In this puddle of darkness
Even the trees listen

To a violin sinking into the rain
And the puddle my heart

Splashes through like a child
With new shoes and no memories

Of loss. We came here to lose
Parts of ourselves

We'll leave with all the music
Our hearts can hold.

DIXIE SALAZAR has previously published four books of poetry: *Altar for Escaped Voices, Voices of the Wind, Flamenco Hips and Red Mud Feet, Hotel Fresno, Reincarnation of the Commonplace* (winner of the National Poetry Book Award), and *Blood Mysteries.* She has also published a novel, *Limbo,* and *Carmen and Chia Mix Magic,* a young adult novel. Her work has appeared in more than fifty literary journals, including *The Missouri Review, Poetry International,* and *Ploughshares.* She currently shows oil paintings and collage work at the Silva/Salazar studios in Fresno. She has taught at California State University, Fresno, as well as in the California prisons and the Fresno County jail.

Printed in the USA
CPSIA information can be obtained
at www.ICGtesting.com
JSHW020747120923
48066JS00008B/23

9 781622 882427